QUANTUM LEADERSHIP

DARE
TO
SEE
THINGS
DIFFERENTLY

NANCY LLOYD, Ph.D.

BALBOA.
PRESS

A DIVISION OF HAY HOUSE

Balboa Press books may be ordered through booksellers or by contacting:

Balboa Press
A Division of Hay House
1663 Liberty Drive
Bloomington, IN 47403
www.balboapress.com
1 (877) 407-4847

Printed in the United States of America.

ISBN: 978-1-4525-8520-8 (sc)
ISBN: 978-1-4525-8521-5 (e)

Balboa Press rev. date: 11/26/2013

EPIGRAPH

"You don't have to hold a position to be a leader."

Henry Ford, founder of Ford Motor Company

"To be a leader you must hold a position of personal responsibility; a response to ability."

Nancy Lloyd, Ph.D.

ABOUT THE AUTHOR

Dr. Nancy earned her Ph.D. in Transpersonal Psychology from Delphi University in Georgia and has been involved in the study of discovering and creating thought connections between the left and right brain and beyond for most of her life.

She has held management and leadership positions in small and large health care related organizations for more than 30 years. During that time she has coached and mentored others in "seeing" things differently. She is currently holding a management/leadership position in a world-wide humanitarian organization.

She resides in North Carolina with her Calico Cat Companion, Lexie and enjoys traveling, reading, and finding laughter and magic in everyday life.

<u>PREFACE</u>

I see things differently. The organization I have been deeply involved with for many years has been struggling and I could feel the tension rising. I went to bed one night thinking about the situation and wondering what I could "do" differently to be a part of the solution to the struggle.

That night I had a dream/vision that summed things up in a way that frightened me. The vision was of two hands gripping a pickle jar; one hand holding the bottom and one holding the top. The lid was being tightened to the point where I knew either the jar would break or the hands holding it would break. And I knew what I could do to be part of the solution.

When the pain of the circumstance you are in becomes greater than the pain of changing the circumstance, you are sufficiently motivated to make the change regardless of the cost.

It was time for me to face my fears and embrace who I am. I see and feel things differently and that has not always been pleasant or well received.

I have faced many fears in writing this book, some of which you will read about. I have embraced who I am, what I see and how I feel with the support of family, friends and teachers. I cherish the knowledge gained from those who have shown me love and those that have caused me pain.

I have been told many times that I am a good teacher. I have used this ability subtly all my life. I am a good teacher, not because I tell you what I think you need to know. I am a good teacher because I guide you to what you want to know.

__INTRODUCTION__

Do you know how to cook a frog? You put the frog in a pot of water that is cool and then bring the temperature up slowly. As the water warms, the frog is lulled into a trance-like state and doesn't even notice that the water is getting hotter and hotter. By the time the frog notices, if it ever does, it is too late.

Why tell this story? My career was in a comfortable sleep state and I thought I would just cruise into retirement at that point. I had been lulled into the status quo for several years. My focus was on taking care of my aging mother and working to make a living. I was mentally exhausted.

With her passing in 2010, I slowly realigned my focus back to work and career. When planned major changes within the organization seemed like a reality and I was offered a chance to be a part of it, I said yes with open arms. It was exactly what I needed to recharge my batteries, so to speak.

I have had the knowledge to create change for many years, but did not feel the openness within the organization as a whole to share my knowledge. As you will read in the book, I had my personal challenges with coming forward also.

However, my knowledge did not go to waste. I was working with my team, with the management in my particular center and found them to be open to some of my different ideas. It allowed me to venture into new territory with the manager and supervisors and set expectations higher for all of us. When much of the regional management changed in 2012, I felt a breath of fresh air come into our organization and I started "feeling the call" to offer more of myself.

As you will read later, self sabotage kept me from doing more within the organization as a whole, even though I continued to do things with my team, with center management and the supervisors. I did things that would make people think, take responsibility, and refocus on the positive side of things.

By 2013 I felt the change in the Earth's atmosphere and the organizational atmosphere so strongly that I had to do more with what I have to offer.

Remember what I said earlier? When the pain of where you are, is greater than the pain of change, you are then sufficiently motivated to effect the change.

I decided to write this book for a change. May it be a catalyst for Quantum Leadership and Quantum Success in your organization.

Nancy Lloyd, Ph.D.

CONTENTS

1.   Turning Trauma to Treasure   1

2.   Embracing Energetic Intelligence: 11

3.   Bridging States of Mind   31

4.   Building Brain Bridges   47

5.   Developing Focus, Feelings and Faith   75

6.   Refining Goals and Measurements   93

7.   The Focus Forum   103

8.   Insight on Intention   109

9.   Conclusion   119

<u>CHAPTER 1</u>

<u>*Turning Trauma to Treasure*</u>

At the age of 18 I was on going on a date. I hadn't dated a lot in high school and that made this date very meaningful to me. It was Christmas time and I was full of anticipation. He picked me up at my parent's house and we went to a Christmas party/dance. I was all "done up" with the make-up and hair done perfectly, decked out in my brown velvet dress with a high lacy collar and long sleeves. My pretty brown heels finished off the "look" beautifully. I was so happy. The party was fun, the band was great, and we danced for hours. The food was good and the wine flowed freely. All seemed perfect and I was enjoying myself with this man.

It was on the ride home that the evening took a dramatic turn. Without my consent, he pulled the car into a vacant parking lot in an industrial area and there demanded more than I was willing to provide. I was inexperienced with how to handle this situation and did not handle it well. The word "No" did not work; scratching and screaming did not work; trying to get away did not work. I escaped from the car only once to be caught and thrown back into the car. I was beaten up, raped, and strangled into silence. I sat in silence, suffering in great shock as he drove me home and I felt him watching me as I numbly got out of the car. I did not look back.

I spent the next few hours in shock, showering and crying. I felt shame, remorse, humiliation, pain, terror, anger, stupidity, and finally exhaustion. But in that new state of exhaustion, there came a surrendering state of mind. I asked for understanding and comfort, but not in the way most would do in this circumstance.

You see I did not believe in a vengeful God; I did not believe in random acts of violence; I did not believe in the fickle finger of fate. I did not ask God "Why me?" I did not ask God to harm him.

I asked, "How do things like this happen to seemingly innocent people? How do people get what they get in life? Why do some people experience certain things and others get to experience other things? How does life work? How do I get off this merry-go-round? I asked that last question, not out of conscious understanding at that point. I asked from an unconscious, yet poignant understanding that another male had attempted to rape me when I was only 4 or 5 years old. I did not consciously remember that until I was 50. The merry-go-round represented the same events, but with different people; a pattern in my life that I wanted to change.

This was the moment in my life when I started turning the trauma into treasure.

And so the journey of discovering self and Universal Energy began. Slowly I was given insight into my life and how this pattern started taking shape. I flashed back to a memory of being a little girl "put to bed" while my parents had company. I could hear their conversation while they were playing a card game. In this flashback, I could hear my father say that his greatest fear in having a daughter was that she would be raped, and all of the others entered into the conversation. I didn't even know what the word meant then, but I knew it had to be bad because of the hushed and serious tones of those talking. Our parents have great influence over our lives and do the best they can with the knowledge they have. My father's fear was out of love for me and wanting me to be safe and happy.

What he did not know and what took me years to find out is:

Focus + Feelings = Formation

Beyond flashbacks for understanding at that time, my mother and grandmother would try to help me cope with what had happened. Being raped and being in counseling were unwanted "stigmas" in those days so I just "dealt" with it the best I could.

Being stoic women who had dealt with their own traumas over the years, my mother and grandmother would say things like, "You can spend your life running *from* things, or you can spend your life running *toward* things. One produces a life of fear, pain and exhaustion: one produces a life of expectation, fulfillment and expansion."

Great advice, not always easy to follow, but I learned to "walk away" from the trauma. I kept learning from my experiences what worked and didn't work. I kept asking questions of my mother, grandmother, myself and the Universe. I kept choosing to see things differently as a result of these influences and my inherent nature. I learned to look deeper and longer at my experiences.

Life Experience:

When two supervisors where I worked chose to malign me and spread false rumors about me, I asked for insight about their behavior. I was able to recognize their jealousy and insecurity. I then chose to treat them with kindness and keep doing the best I could do. I would smile and say hello to them even though they repeatedly snubbed me. Later in our careers, these same two supervisors *needed me* to advance their careers. I could have been vindictive, but because I was able to see them differently, I chose to build them up and help them advance. Imagine the anguish they had to have experienced when faced with the task of having to ask me for help! Choosing the road less traveled allowed me to grow.

*

I learned lessons by experimenting with more questions. What is my next step in advancing my career? I followed my inspiration and decided to apply for a job I didn't really want, but it was close by and would give me good interviewing experience. I saw the interviews going well and them loving me. I interviewed with many people over two days and they offered me the job. Even though it was not the end career move I originally wanted, I took the job for the experience. I learned so much from that position that helped me for many years to come.

*

That worked so well that I decided to just keep asking questions: How do I get the next job I want? I was inspired again and moved up the ladder with that next position and again with the next position. I kept listening for the answers and feeling the energetic nudges and taking inspired action.

*

By that time I was studying more about how the Universe worked and I was applying my knowledge to even more situations. Even though I did not have my Master's degree at the time, all of this gave me the audacity to apply for THE ONE position I had wanted from the age of 15. The position required it, but with all of my experience, I was given the position without it.

At the age of 15, however, I now realize I was chasing the title and the salary and not focusing clearly on all of the details I truly wanted in that position. After three years in it, I was feeling overwhelmed and unhappy; working 12 hour days, 6 days a week, never getting the job done the way I wanted and never feeling like there was enough time to handle all of the priorities. I was in the depths of despair over this very position that I had wanted for years! What to do next?

I asked another powerful question, "How do I get out of this mess and heal myself?" I fantasized about how much paid annual leave I had accumulated and how I could use that. I fantasized about severance pay and unemployment benefits. I didn't really **want** to get fired; I just wanted out and at that level of exhaustion and despair, it was the only option I could see. I was so deep in the problem that I could not see clearly and not able to see a good solution. I felt desperate!

Well, I was now a really good creator in my life. I "forgot" in my despair that my focus and my feelings were creating what I wanted (to get out) but not in a way I **really wanted!** I got fired! Not only did I get fired, but the cause listed on my record was for "lack of leadership"! OUCH! OUCH! OUCH! OUCH! OUCH! OUCH! Through my tears I was asking myself different questions. "Are you crazy? What have you done to yourself? Have you forgotten everything you know to be true? Now what are you going to do?"

Focus + Feelings = Formation

I did get what I focused on: I was allowed to work a 6 week notice, get severance pay, use my 3 months of paid annual leave, and get unemployment benefits, a good reference and outplacement counseling! It sort of felt like the consolation prize at that point, but as I reflected I had to admit that I had done a good job of formation, good job of focusing, good job of creating strong feelings, *but not such a good job of being aware of creating from a negative state of mind!*

Be careful what level of mind you are creating from: a creation is still a creation.

*

Experience is a great and grand teacher. And the fact is we are always creating our lives, personally and professionally, by default or by design, by one state of mind or another. We are also influencing the same for others that work with us or live with us!

The key is to know how things work and use the knowledge to your advantage.

All of the events of your life can be turning points. In small boat sailing, we would put a piece of yarn through the sail at strategic points. The way the yarn flew on the sail would tell us whether we needed to adjust the direction of the boat or the set of the sails in order to use the wind to our best advantage and get where we wanted to be in the most efficient time. The pieces of yarn are called "tell tails". I was learning to focus my direction and my state of mind to my advantage.

When I raced sailboats, a fellow competitor gave me some great advice. I asked him why he was so successful at winning races and he answered this way. All of us make mistakes in the race and the wind is always shifting. It is those of us who notice our mistakes and the shifting winds first, who then make the necessary corrections and change the set of our sails first that win the races. He may have been sorry he told me that. I beat him the very next race!

__The Winds of Fate__

One ship drives east and another drives west

With the selfsame winds that blow.

'Tis the set of the sails

And not the gales

Which tell us the way to go.

Like the winds of the sea are the ways of fate,

As we voyage along through life:

'Tis the set of a soul

That decides its goal,

And not the calm or the strife.

Ella Wheeler Wilcox

CHAPTER 2

Embracing Energetic Intelligence:

The Importance of Understanding Your World

Life Experience:

I was at a seminar once of about 100 people from different states and different backgrounds. Very few people knew each other and most just took their seats waiting for the seminar to start. This was a personal growth seminar that attracted a variety of people.

After we were seated the instructor asked those people who were in the teaching field to stand up. About 20 people stood; all of whom were sitting fairly close to each other. When asked if they knew each other, only one or two were acquaintances.

The instructor then asked them to sit down and asked if those in the medical field would stand up. About 30 people stood and they seemed to be in a cluster on the other side of the room. When asked if they knew each other, only a small fraction knew one other person in the group.

The instructor continued with other professions and the same "grouping" seemed to be evident even when people did not know each other.

This is an example of cognitive resonance; when people hold the same beliefs, ideas, values, attitudes, emotional reactions and energy fields. Very few people in this group knew each other, yet they unknowingly grouped themselves together through their energy fields. They gravitated toward their comfort zones and gravitated away from those not in congruence or resonance. Those in specific occupations have a specific way of looking at things; have their own language and even general types of personalities. Our energy fields hold not just our professional resonance, but any number of things like economic, sexual, educational, and ethnic customs, beliefs, attitudes and comfort zones. The list goes on and on.

*

A psychologist once told me of a study that involved an abused woman who was put in a room with 100 men. Ninety-nine of these men were gentle, caring and respectful men and 1 was an abuser. This abused woman managed to gravitate to the abuser within minutes of entering that room and stayed with him until called out of the room. She had cognitive resonance with being abused and felt most comfortable with the abuser. Her basis of belief was that abuse was normal, so it was most comfortable for her to be with the abuser.

*

I recently went to a gathering of about 25 people that I knew. I was offered some water when I arrived and sat at the kitchen counter as I sipped on it. A man approached that I dreaded talking to. He focuses on the negative and feels everyone is conspiring against him. I put up with it for a while, then excused myself and went to the restroom.

As I was washing my hands, I looked in the mirror and asked myself, "What did I do to attract that?" The answer came to me immediately. I was in counseling mode. In counseling, I listen to others dump their negative "stuff" and then I redirect or refocus them to a positive perspective. It is what I do in my professional life. In a social situation like this, however, I was not a counselor and redirecting was not appropriate with this man. He wasn't asking for help. He just wanted to dump his "stuff."

Well, I could have been angry with him for messing up what was supposed to be an enjoyable day with these people. I could have tried to avoid him for the rest of the day, but this was a small house and I wasn't sure I could do that effectively. The fact was "my beliefs," energy field, or state of mind had just mirrored themselves to me "in person." Trying to fix the mirror or avoid it would simply not fix the problem.

I had to change my belief or my energy field so that my mirror of belief was that which I desired. I decided at that moment to be in social mode on this day and expect a relaxing day of pleasant conversation and to put my counseling mode on the back burner in my mind. It took 2-3 minutes while I was in the restroom to do this.

When I came back into the living room, that man was not anywhere to be seen. He had moved to another area, and I did not run into him, nor did he seek me out for the rest of the 5 to 6 hours that I was there. Yahoo!

Your Energy Field and The Mirror

What the above illustrations demonstrate is that we wear our attitudes, beliefs, values, and emotions and even our professions like a coat. They are in the energy field that surrounds us. Others feel them, sense them, and react to them knowingly or not. Looking at events as a mirror of the energy field and those attitudes, beliefs, etc is an awareness tool for you to know yourself better and know your own resonance/vibration. It is so unconsciously a part of you that you don't know you are radiating it until it bounces back to you as a mirror from some other person or event in your life or in your work.

Are you happy with your mirror? When you are unhappy with your mirror, do you try to fix the mirror? Do you put a bandage on it; do you avoid looking at it; do you scratch at it? In other words, do you blame others, society, and events for your situation?

You cannot fix the problem reflected in the mirror by attacking the mirror. You have to change your energy field, your attitudes, beliefs, etc., before you will see a change in others, events, and your environment.

In order to create more effectively in your life and your business, you must become aware of your mirrors and know how to change yourself to change the mirror.

Have you ever heard someone say, "I'll believe it when I see it?" The thing is, what you already believe is what you are seeing. You see what you believe because formation/creation is based on your focus and your feelings/emotions.

It's not the way we were taught to look at things, is it? We did not know the formula, because most of our parents, teachers and preachers did not know it. If you believe what you were taught by them, then you are unconsciously creating by default. You are creating what they taught you to create because you have "bought into" their beliefs out of ignorance of how creation works. Creating by default rather than by design is the result of lack of knowledge, lack of belief, or lack of focus in general.

Formation/Creation is not believing it when you see it, but seeing it when you believe it.

- Focus is the direction of the Formation.

- Feelings are the catalyst of the Formation.

- Faith is the glue that pulls the Formation together.

Your Energy Field Frequencies and the Frequencies of the Earth

Dr. Celeste De Bease, PhD, is board certified in biofeedback and neurofeedback. She is an associate professor and director of biofeedback at Widener University and explains brain waves at varying electrical frequencies measured in hertz (cycles per second). Using this knowledge, many of her clients have been helped to focus on performance enhancement, including athletes, business professionals and members of the military.

Delta – 1 to 3 Hz, the slowest of all, is mostly seen during sleep.

Theta – 4 to 7 Hz, a state of deep relaxation that can bring bursts of creative insight. It occurs during daydreaming and advanced meditation.

Alpha – 8 to 13 Hz, a pleasurable, relaxed state associated with being calm and lucid. It occurs in some forms of meditation and sometimes with dream sleep.

Beta – 14-30 Hz, the frequency produced during normal waking activities, when you are processing information for daily living.

High Beta – any Beta over 21 Hz, showing that the brain is in its racing mode associated with anxiety and tension.

How do our brain waves and energy fields relate to the global electromagnetic energy fields/resonances?

Earth Frequencies

According to the Schumann Resonance study in 1952, the Earth has had a base frequency of 7.8 hertz for many years and has recently been increasing. It is now believed that in 2013 it has risen to 13.0 hertz.

The Earth is part of a Universal Harmonic field and frequencies bounce or echo back when sent or radiated out into this field. Radio waves are sent out into the "air" or harmonic field and are echoed back.

That is how our radios can pick up signals from great distances away. Our own brains, in the form of thoughts and emotions, also send or radiate out into the "air", or the Universal Harmonic field, and they are echoed back to us. We "see" it in the "mirror" as I described earlier. What we see through our beliefs is echoed back to us.

If you look at the previous information about brain waves and do a little comparison, it is almost as if the Earth and our brains have been synced up in a state of deep relaxation with only occasional creative insights for many years in the 7.8Hz range.

Yet the Earth's frequency has risen to about 13 Hz which corresponds to an awakening of the brain and to a state of lucidity and clear focus. Alpha brain waves most match up with the new frequency of the Earth, and this is also the state of lucidity.

Jose Silva, Creator of the Silva Mind Development Programs, states that," you have to learn to function in alpha brain waves to be certain that most of your decisions will be correct ones. During the day the brain dips into the alpha level an average of about 30 times per minute. This happens naturally and it seems to happen for everybody. But the time in alpha is very short, only microseconds. In all, the brain may be in alpha five seconds out of every minute. It is during these times that people are able to be certain of making clear decisions, decisions that will help correct problems. Maybe that is why the average person, who does not know how to function at the alpha level when desired, is correct only twenty percent of the time."

The change in the Earth's resonating vibrational/ energetic field may be disconcerting, confusing, and can create chaos for many. If a person does not know how to achieve more alpha brain wave activity and use the information for positive change, it certainly can create a spacey feeling and confusion.

I look at some of the changes that have taken place in the world in the years leading up to 2013 and can see the chaos. Economies have collapsed and some businesses have collapsed or are on the verge of it. Massive weather pattern changes, mass murders, a fascination with mind-numbing drugs, hallucinogens, and violent movies and games speak to the chaos.

Perhaps you have experienced some of these things or at least have been touched by these things in your own lives and the businesses you manage/lead. I hear people asking" What is going on?"

As we move into this different frequency on Earth and the world is working at a different pace than most of us are accustomed to, we don't understand our own brain frequencies, and we may not know where to get answers or how to adjust. The old patterns and fixes just don't work anymore, but we are not sure how to change old patterns or create new approaches and solutions.

The good news is that we can develop our brain wave frequencies to sync up with the Earth's and come into harmonic balance with more lucidity and get out of a sleep state. We must however, learn how to function more frequently in the alpha brain wave state in order to do so and create what is desired and not keep creating by default or ignorance.

Mohandas Gandhi, *"First they ignore you. Then they laugh at you. Then they fight you. Then you win."*

I know this may sound like a foreign language to most reading this, yet it is the language you and I have been living with all of our lives. Just like we live with the gravitational field whether we understand it or not, we live with these frequencies whether we understand it or not.

When we begin to understand it, however, we begin to use it to our advantage. The language of frequency/vibration and energy fields is how we actually communicate with the Universe and to learn it and use it gives us an advantage in creating the life we want. It mirrors back to us in our life and our business each and every moment. Could you use a change in your life or your business?

"Everyone thinks of changing the world, but no one thinks of changing himself." - Leo Tolstoy

Gregg Braden, computer systems designer and New York Times best-selling author of *The Spontaneous Healing of Belief*, states that his book was written with one purpose in mind: to share an empowering message of hope and possibility in a world where we are often led to feel hopeless and powerless. He goes into great detail about our vibrational universe and quantum physics.

For example:

Belief Code 1. Experiments show that the focus of our attention changes reality itself and suggests that we live in an interactive universe.

Belief Code 2. We live our lives based on what we believe about our world, ourselves, our capabilities and our limits.

What does all of this talk about frequencies mean to you and me?

It means that our resonant frequencies must change to be in harmony with the universal energy in order to live our lives most effectively and perform our jobs/responsibilities more effectively; to lead by design and not by default.

These concepts are real. Science is proving what many of us have felt and known for years. The Earth is a vibrational place and so is everything in it, including each of us. Our focus and feelings ARE our vibrational frequencies and we must learn to use them effectively. They make up our energy field.

Translation: We create our "space/life/careers" on this earth based on how we focus and how we feel about what we are focusing on now and now and now and again now in this very moment. Focus + Feelings = Formation in each and every moment.

Panche Desai, developer of *Awakening your Passion, Power and Infinite Potential* and student of the universe, states:

"How You Vibrate Is What The Universe Echoes Back To You In Every Moment."

What are you vibrating/feeling/thinking right now? What is your energy field broadcasting right now? Do you ever vibrate the feelings of boredom, fear, doubt, anger, hatred, frustration, irritation, impatience, or being overwhelmed? What are you thinking/focusing on when you feel these things? The result of the focus and feeling creates an out-picturing or mirror of this in your life.

Do you ever vibrate the feelings of love, compassion, positive expectation, belief, optimism, contentment, and hopefulness? What are you thinking/focusing on when you feel these things? Once again, you will observe that there is an out-picturing or mirror of this in your life.

Is it always instant? No. But when it becomes a general vibrational resonance or energy field you will notice a trend in your life, in your relationships and in your work. Be mindful of your mirrors. Start to notice trends in your experiences.

Where do you "generally" vibrate on the emotional scale about your life, your relationships, and your work? Do you ever blame others for what is going on in your life or business; as in the government, economy, regulations, family, friends, employees, media? The fact is each of us is responsible for what is happening to us. We love taking the responsibility when things are going well, but tend to point fingers when things are not going so well! After all, you wouldn't create negative events on purpose; would you? Enter default conditioned mass thinking. We do it without awareness in most instances because it is what we have been taught by those we believed in and listened to in our homes, schools, and societies.

Many of us do not vibrate on a pleasurable, relaxed state of lucidity frequency as a general rule. We have been steeped in the fears, tears and beliefs of our parents, teachers and preachers. We are bombarded by the media and influenced by our governments. We have been in a trance and settled into the vibrational frequency that was in harmony with our Earth in the sleep state. The collective energy created that environment, and we contributed to it through ignorance for the most part!

We either are not aware or we have forgotten that we create our lives in each and every moment: that we are at this moment creating our futures. And now we have a better chance of creating them with lucidity if we are willing to change and learn the process of getting up to speed with the new frequencies.

Mike Dooley, New York Times Best-Selling author of *Infinite Possibilities,* shares his ideas in the book as a fresh and inspiring look at how each of us can turn within to discover our true purpose, ignite our imagination, and manifest our desires. He writes Notes from the Universe giving new perspectives on life.

One Example:

Do you think gravity has to work twice as hard to hold an elephant to the ground as it does an acorn? Ha. So please understand, it's the same with the principle of "thoughts become things." The size of your dream has nothing to do with the likelihood of them coming to pass, nothing. Think BIG.

"Thoughts become things... pick the good ones." ®

How Can We Use This in Business?

When we discuss this in a business connotation, we can look at the organization in different ways. Most just see the mainstream workforce, management, events, processes and products in the organization as facts, figures, one or two dimensional entities.

I see things differently. A business entity is an organism, organ and then an organization to me. A business organization is a living, breathing thing to me. It has its own harmonic field influenced by its owners/

leaders. That means that it also has focus and feelings/ emotions attached to it that are also influenced by its owner/leaders, its beliefs/credos, and the demands of society much as each individual is.

The general functioning of an organization is living and breathing and often exhibits the ills of any organism from time to time. This comes from a basis of faulty thinking, beliefs, and emotions about a particular part or function of the organism. As with any organism, it must be treated holistically. Fixing one problem does not fix the whole organism. If an organism is composed of (M)ental, (E)motional, (S)piritual and (P)hysical characteristics and you only deal with the Physical or P in the equation then you have left out the M, E, and S of the equation. You are left with a **MES(S)** in my opinion. I see things differently.

It stands to reason then, that in order to change an organization or fix a problem within the organization, that we must use different thinking, different emotions/ feelings, and a different level of vibration than what created the problem in the first place. We must explore other possibilities to find solutions to problems. We need to create thoughts and emotions that serve our organism/organization and then move the energy to a level at which we can achieve the results we desire.

Mark Twain wrote:

"The man with a new idea is a crank until the idea succeeds."

"There is no other life; life itself is only a vision and a dream, for nothing exists but space and you."

CHAPTER 3

Bridging States of Mind

"We cannot solve our problems with the same thinking we used when we created them."

Albert Einstein

As I see it, different states of the mind correlate with the different characteristics of the brain and that gives us a greater understanding to function more effectively in problem solving. Let's take a look at the Left brain, the Right brain, and the Genius brain.

Left Brain

In the **Left brain,** the mind is generally associated with:

- focusing on logical, linear, and detail oriented material,

- having a grounded and facts only focus,

- organizing and **making** things happen with action,

- saying "but" when presented with issues,

- looking for things that can work and for things that can't work,

- having a higher (14-30 Hz) frequency area of the brain,

- focusing on normal waking activities and information processing,

- being foundational, necessary, and generally associated with masculine energy,

- being the producer or giver to the world,

- making strong **Managers,**

- dealing with probabilities,

- having a "the world needs me" attitude.

The Left Brain produces the facts, the data and the foundation for an organization. It produces the management style of dealing with only facts and figures and that which is physical or literal. In many organizations, it is often the ONLY state of mind used to run the business. If a problem is perceived here in the Left Brain, grounded state of mind, it is not the state of mind best suited for finding or creating the solution. It looks for solutions using only the facts it knows to be true.

Doing the same things over and over and expecting different results is the definition of insanity.

Albert Einstein

Right Brain

In the **Right brain** the mind is generally associated with:

- focusing on fun, art, creativity, recreation, and vision,

- relaxing and **letting** things happen with the flow of focused energy,

- being generative and expansive and inspiring new perspectives,

- having a lower (13 Hz) frequency and associated with alpha brain waves,

- being more relaxed, lucid, pleasurable and calm,

- being the visionary and generally associated with feminine energy,

- using "and" statements, rather than "but" statements,

- being the creator or receiver from the world,

- loving to search for answers,

- staying subtle, often sensed as "gut feelings," intuition, and nudges

- making strong **Leaders,**

- dealing with possibilities,

- having "the world needs a muse" attitude.

The Right brain is where many new and creative ideas come from when looking for solutions to problems. It is able to finesse facts and data in new ways to come up with completely new approaches. It coaxes the energy to move instead of staying rigid. The Right brain is the, "I have a bright idea" side of the mind that ignore probabilities and seeks possibilities.

It is important to understand that organizations need people with both strong managerial **and** leadership skills to function well. They need Right brained people and Left brained people and more and more they need whole brained people to create the synthesis needed between the two.

During the last few years I have observed many organizations changing people in management and leadership positions to add new perspectives and to create new solutions. This can work out well if the organization is **open** to this new "state of mind" thinking and perspectives that these new people bring with them. When these people are brought in to a predominately Left brained organization and they hear a lot of "buts" and "probabilities", it can stifle their creativity and they can become frustrated, exhausted and jaded over time. They lose that new perspective they came in with and begin to create by default again. They begin to conform because Left brain dominance can be perceived as bullying by the more sensitive Right brained person.

The Right brain is more likely to take a back seat in this situation and conform rather than fight the Left brain. The Right brain is a lover, not a fighter.

Whole brained people are impassioned people, and they work best when empowered by an organization that can embrace the "new" as well as the "old" attitudes. An organization that is open to the kind of people that use "and" when searching for solutions, can assess the "buts" when looking at issues and come up with solutions that blend the probabilities with the possibilities. Adding the Right brained kind of approach to the organizational problems moves the "solution process" to another state of mind than that which created the problem. When these Whole Brained people are empowered and supported, the organization has a better chance of, not just surviving, but thriving.

Newton's Law

The cure is not just action; it is engaging the Universal Action or Positional Advantage. Using not only our left brain, but engaging the right brain creativity and vision.

Bridging the gap between the Left brain and the Right brain is critical and yet sometimes difficult if someone has never done it and has no idea how to do it.

Life Experience:

I have been career oriented my entire life and primarily functioned from my Left brain in everyday business issues. I worked in Left brain

type of organizations and fell into the default thinking already established. I knew that if I was to grow as a leader, I had to learn how to bridge the gap and use my Right brain in spite of the dominant organizational energy field.

(Remember: I was fired once for lack of leadership ability?)

I was working with a specialized therapist to help me in this process. I see concepts visually and when directed I visualized my Left brain as a male and my Right brain as a female. Turns out this was not a pleasant vision!

They, this male and female, were standing on opposite sides of the Grand Canyon, each on a ledge and each facing the opposite direction; one looking north and the other looking south. They did not even know the other existed.

My therapist was helping to get the two of them talking and,

eventually we got them to look at each other. But they each had a look of disdain on their faces. They did not recognize each other, obviously did not like each other, did not respect each other and did not trust each other! OUCH!

After much talking to reach an understanding between them and getting nowhere, my therapist directed me to create a bridge and we convinced this male and female to start crossing the bridge to meet in the middle. They did so with great reluctance and a lot of coaching.

When they reached the middle, they had little to say to each other.

But in my therapist's infinite wisdom, he suggested that I create an earthquake and so I did just that.

As the earth shook and the bridge swayed uncontrollably, the male and female grabbed each other and the bridge. They decided that misery loves company, better to die with someone than to die alone!

By the time the earth and bridge stopped moving, they started talking. They had shared a trauma and now had somewhere to start a conversation.

They ultimately decided that it was nice to have company, someone to talk to and share ideas with! After a time they were laughing

*and talking at breakneck speed and deciding
on all the things they could do together!*

*He had great focus, and she had great creativity.
Together they thought they could move mountains.*

So for those reading who are not as stubborn as I was and are not inclined to seek a specialized therapist to create the bridge, I will offer alternatives later in the book. You might find this explanation a bit more relatable:

The Left brain and Right brain decide to go to a 5 star steak house for dinner one night. They order the steak they want with mashed potatoes and green beans. Their order is now in the hands of the chef and all the people that make a restaurant run (the Genius brain and all the resources of the universe).

They don't worry about the order; they know it will show up and be perfect. When their order does show up, everything they ordered is on the plate as expected. What was not expected was the presentation. The steak is in the center of the plate with the mashed potatoes and green beans artfully placed on top of the steak with a show of great creatively.

Left brain - The Chef is an Idiot!

Right brain - The Chef is a Genius!

The Left brain stares at this "mess" and is very disturbed. While the basics are present, the order is something not expected. In fact there is no order at all. The Left brain wants everything in order and in separate spaces. It starts to create order on the plate, putting everything in its proper space and then and only then, can it enjoy the experience.

The Right brain stares at this "work of art" and savors the creativity. It relishes the aroma and enjoys the sound of the sizzling steak; it anticipates the wonderful flavor. It loves the unique way the basic elements are presented and dives into the experience with the joy of a new experience.

The Genius brain (to be discussed next) looks on without judgment, knowing that differing views are needed for structure and creativity. Harmony and synthesis begins when the Left brain and Right brain can appreciate and respect each other's different perspectives and approaches to the same situation. If they start to argue, judge or disrespect each other's views, no harmony or synthesis exists and an internal battle ensues that prevents problem solving and creative leadership.

The creation of the bridge between the states
of mind is critical to effective problem-
solving and creative leadership.

Consider these questions:

- Have you ever had a great idea that you never acted on, never manifested? Right brain talking; Left brain not listening!

- Have you ever felt stuck in a problem and searched for inspiration, but none came? Left brain talking, Right brain not listening!

It is necessary to create a partnership of respect and trust between the Right and Left brain. If you have ever conducted personality or leadership type testing in your organization, you found that some people learn slowly and some fast, some lead by immersion and some by observation, some prefer to engage with paper/computers, while others enjoy engaging with people. Some people need all the facts to make a decision, while others only major points to make a decision. But don't you need all types to accomplish all the facets of your business. Isn't it critical that people respect and trust each other's strengths?

That is what needs to happen in your own brain. All the players are needed to be effective, let alone excellent. They play to the strengths of each other and use them together to create a greater whole. You can more easily handle all the facets of your business/organization and have access to a way of solving problems more quickly when everything is synced up.

Genius Brain

There is another state of mind that can make leadership even more dynamic and powerful to achieve greater results with less effort and harness vibrational or universal energy. It is called the Genius brain.

The Genius brain is the state of mind associated with:

- having theta brain waves at even lower (4-7 Hz) frequencies,

- being the state of mind associated with deep relaxation,

- bringing bursts of creative insight flooding into your consciousness,

- creating states of lucid daydreaming,

- allowing lucid meditation, and subconscious creation,

- creating synchronicities in life and work,

- creating the serendipities (unexpected pleasant events),

- and true harmony,

- forgoing judgment,

- having a "the world needs to use all available resources" attitude.

Creating an additional bridge to the one created from the Left brain to the Right brain, it allows a person to become a Whole brained person *and* a Quantum Leader.

People like this are the ultimate visionaries, using their creative powers to change outcomes with vibrational energy by using all of the resources available to them.

Those who engage the Genius brain are the **Quantum Leaders.** They are the mentors, the coaches, the counselors, and the gurus. They are the people who say "What if" and come up with possibilities, expectations, visions and a "knowing" that is intuitive.

When you engage the Genius brain, you engage the most creative part of you in harmony with the universal energies that are echoing back to you all of the time. You simply have to be in a state of mind to receive.

- **The Genius brain is the part that knows infinite possibilities.**

Bringing this to an organizational level would create a paradigm shift for the leadership of the organization and create a "whole state of mind" which is required for greatest effectiveness. An organization, just like the body, is most effective when all means of wholeness and health are explored and used to benefit all.

This paradigm shift is critical at the leadership level and the effects trickle out to all involved just like the ripples created by one pebble being dropped into a still pond affect the entire pond. The ripples will reach the other shore and the other shore will not even know why it is experiencing ripples, but it will feel them and respond. Many leaders making this paradigm shift can create a tidal wave effect in an organization!

It has been estimated that 1 hour of Right brain work is equal to 2000 hours of Left brain work. Imagine what could be accomplished with the addition of the Genius brain and the creation of a "whole brain state of mind"!

Whole brain leadership is needed to maintain, grow and make organizations viable in the new energies evolving on Earth and in the Universe.

I see it this way: The Synchronization of Formation

- The Genius brain is the light source.

- The Right brain receives and molds it with joy.

- The Left brain focuses it with laser precision.

CHAPTER 4

Building Brain Bridges

It's important to know where you are starting from when building brain bridges. Let's find out what your customary leadership style is and you will know what bridges need to be developed.

Customary Leadership Style

Anyone who has been in a management or leadership position for any length of time comes into the position having already learned many techniques from many sources. Some learned their management techniques from parents, from teachers, friends, or pure observation of others. Some have taken the time to take courses or read books and adapt the leadership style of the teachers or incorporate them with the ones already working.

You have an adopted customary leadership style, which is the blending of all of your experiences and education together. In the following exercise or process you will find out what your "intuitive" customary leadership style is - your comfort zone.

Read through the process so you know what you are doing and then proceed. Do this for about 1-2 minutes and then jot down all of the details.

Exercise:

You need to be sitting in a quiet area where you will be undisturbed for a few minutes. Close your eyes. Take a few deep breaths, in through the nose and out through the mouth. Simply feel a wave of relaxation move down through your body from your head to your feet.

Now visualize a mountain in front of you. You are at the base of the mountain.

- Take note of what the mountain looks like;

- Is it steep?

- Does it stand alone?

- Are there other mountains around it?

- What is the temperature?

- Does it have trees?

- What kind of trees or vegetation?

- How does the air smell?

- Is there air movement of any kind?

- Can you see the top of the mountain, etc.?

Now look around and find that you have a team of others behind you. Your job is to lead this team up the mountain to the top. Go.

DO THIS EXERCISE NOW
BEFORE YOU MOVE ON.

So what was your experience?

- Did you do a planning session first?

- Did you just start walking?

- Did you have transportation?

- Was the journey easy?

- Was it hard?

- Was it both?

- What areas were hardest/easiest?

- Did everyone stay together?

- Did everyone have a role?

- Did you stop along the way?

- Were there things you carried with you?

- Did you meet others along the way?

- Were there people to help?

- Were their road signs?

- Were there roads or paths?

- Did you have to create them?

Write down what you experienced.

DO THIS STEP NOW BEFORE YOU MOVE ON.

Life Experience:

When I did this, I was in a group of eight people. When we finished the exercise, each person took a few minutes to share what he or she experienced. There were many different scenarios, mountains covered with pines, mountains covered in palms, journeys that were terrible struggles, others that were relatively easy, with some stopping to rest along the way, while others kept a steady pace. Some people had help while others did not, some took winding paths and others created roads as they went. In other words, the stories were as varied as the people.

When it came my turn, I was reluctant to share my story. Everyone waited as I hesitated. The instructor encouraged me to share.

I saw a beautiful mountain with pines and snow. I led the team to the gondola, and we all got in and road to the top! The scenery was beautiful, the trip was smooth, and we were all energized when we reached the top.

The other students just stared and/or glared at me. Some were angry; some were amazed; some were jealous.

In reality, knowing your customary leadership style is only revealing your comfort zone. The others' comfort zones were to immerse themselves in the trenches, working alongside their team members and leading from the ground level. I, on the other hand, have a customary leadership style of observation so I have the bigger picture in sight at all time.

I have grown to understand that both types of leadership are needed. I have to push out of my comfort zone to join my team in the trenches so that I understand the details and the issues first hand. The others need to get out of the trenches on a regular basis to take a gondola ride, to see the big picture, to be able to better see what lies ahead and be prepared for it.

We all have our own customary and intuitive leadership style, and we all see our journeys differently. This exercise tells us how we lead others most of the time, look at problems or projects, our speed at handling our responsibilities, the tools we choose to use, the way we sense our environment, etc.

This is an awareness tool that you can use on occasion to remind yourself that you may be stuck in your comfort zone and not seeing some of the things that you would if you jumped out of it on a regular basis. It broadens your sight and can make you more responsive rather than reactive to many situations.

How do you customarily look at these things? Do you lead by immersion or by observation? Do you use both? This awareness of yourself and your style of leadership is a key point as we move forward. Whatever it is, you can open yourself to other perspectives for more understanding and greater leadership.

A further note; immersion is primarily a Left brain function, and observation is a Right brain function in leadership.

Building the Bridges to Different States of Mind

Bridge from Left to Right Brain

Talk It Up

The Left brain is generally accustomed to taking action and making decisions based on the facts and figures as presented logically. It tends to go over the same material again and again. The Left brain likes logic, facts, figures, and no nonsense, if you recall. So begin by accepting where your Left brain thoughts are at the moment without judgment. The Left brain is doing what it does best and will keep searching for a resolution to a problem using the means it has. It is difficult for it to come up with an answer because it only uses what it sees to make decisions. It is the best place to analyze a problem, but not the best place to resolve a problem.

The **Talk It Up** process starts with this:
Accept and Redirect

Listen to the thoughts you are having right now and gently redirect your thoughts from mulling over the problem repeatedly to the knowing that you have had successes in the past with problem solving.

The thoughts may go like this:

I know I am frustrated right now and have to come up with a solution. There is a lot riding on finding a solution, and I just have to find one. I also know that I am not making any headway with this problem at the present moment. I have been working on this problem and feel a lot of pressure to come up with the answer now. I have tried everything I know how to do and nothing is working.

Even though I feel frustrated, I also know that I have had success in the past solving other problems. I just have to recall how I did that. I do remember that the answer came when I least expected it. When was that? Was I in the shower, or driving in my car, or just getting up and walking around, taking a break? I know

*it has worked in the past and I'm willing to try it now.
I'll walk away and get a new perspective.*

At this point, get up and walk around for a minute
or two. Go to the restroom and wash your hands.
Water on the hands relaxes the body and is a symbolic
washing away the problem. (Think about cleaning the
windshield of a car. The washer fluid and the wipers
clear the vision.) Take a few slow, deep breaths in and
out. (Good Respiration can = Inspiration.)

With this process you are starting to cross the bridge
to the Right brain, and you are opening to different
options and solutions that you could not think of with
Left brain functions only.

Step It Up

The Right brain has no need to talk to the Left brain
until it feels appreciated and the Left brain is open to
hearing options. In the Talk It Up process, the Left brain
is starting to cross the bridge, which is the signal to the
Right brain to open and welcome the Left brain problem
as an opportunity to create.

The Step It Up process starts with this:
Distraction and Breathing (Inspiration)

When you come back from the restroom, look at a picture of a loved one, a beloved pet, or a relaxing vacation; look out the window if there is a nice view outside and relax your brain. Continue to take some deep breaths slowly and evenly. Respiration invites Inspiration and continues your journey across the bridge to engage the Right brain. It starts to engage more relaxed and pleasant thoughts and makes room for them. It slows the fast paced thoughts of the Left brain. Literally feel the brain relax inside your skull. When the physical brain relaxes, the energetic brain relaxes. It is like there is space between thoughts as opposed to the density of logical thinking. It is like changing the radio station from hard rock to soft jazz. As you continue to relax your thoughts and your body, you can start asking questions.

- First ask questions you could not possibly have the answer to such as: "What does it feel like to sit on a cloud?" or "How many drops of water are in the Atlantic Ocean?"

Just *notice* that your brain is searching for the answer. Often your eyes elevate upward to about a 30 degree angle when doing this, and they may begin to move from right to left and left to right. Your brain is trying to access information from a higher state of mind, from the past, from the present, from the future. Think of the little flashlight that shows up on a computer screen when searching for a file, moving back and forth. That's what your brain is doing right now. It is searching for the answer. Just relax with the questions. You really don't need an answer to these questions. The reason to do it is to open the search function!

At this point choose an "anchor point" for this "search and answer state of mind." Start with 3 deep breaths and some other signal such as touching 2 fingers of your non-dominant hand together, touching your heart with your hand, touching your earlobe, etc. Use an anchor point that you could use in any situation, and no one else would think it odd! You want to be able to use this anchor point in different situations to be able to elicit lucid thinking even in chaotic situations. Using this anchor point technique can actually slow down your brain waves and open the channel to clearer thoughts and better solutions.

Once you have done that, start asking the questions that you really need answers to. Just ask the questions in the right way. You may not get the answer in that moment, but be open to it when you get it. Just keep asking in order to open up your creative Right brain and the search engine.

- Now what do I mean by asking questions in the RIGHT way?

I hear people ask, "What am I doing wrong?" Let me ask you right now; do you really want to know what you are doing wrong? Do you not already have ample evidence that you are doing something wrong and pretty much what that is? This is a disempowering question that will get you more of what you have been getting. You are asking questions of the creative mind, and it can create more negative or "wrong" events if that is what you are asking for and focusing on! Knowing what you are doing wrong is a great catalyst and creates motivation to change things, but why not seek the change without experiencing more of what you don't want.

What you really want to know is, "What is the easiest, quickest resolution to this problem? What is a sustainable resolution to this problem? How can I be a better problem solver? Why do solutions come easily to me when I open my mind and relax? Why do I surround myself with great people and resources that can help me solve these problems? Who can help me resolve this issue? Why do answers come to me so quickly? Why is it so easy to turn problems into opportunities?

These questions stimulate and engage the search engine and even if you don't know the answers right now, the search engine will continue to look for solutions until it finds the answers and shows you.

The world loves problem solvers – be one!

Open It Up

The Left and Right brains are now fully engaged and the lines of communication have opened up.

The Open It Up process starts with:
Listening without Judgment

When you start asking big questions with great desire, you start the flow of creation. When you first start doing this, the first few responses are like getting the rust out of the pipes. Let the answers start flowing and **do not judge them**. Just let them keep flowing, and the answers keep getting clearer. This is a brainstorming session in your own mind! The search engine and consequent answers have been available all along, but there was no one asking or worse yet, no one listening. Open up the pipes and then listen.

Answers will come to you faster when you move into the Right brain state of mind on a routine basis. You are opening new neural pathways and new frequencies. The more you practice using this area of your brain, the more lucid thinking and great decision making you will experience.

Answers will start coming to you in the shower, in the car, looking at a flame, staring at the ocean, petting the cat or dog, playing with your children, just before you go to sleep, in the middle of the night, just as you are waking up, looking out the window, washing your hands, walking in the park, and a million others places when you have relaxed your mind! At first it may take a little time to start getting answers, but as you practice, the answers will be there.

Always have paper and pen handy or at least a way to record the information you are getting. If I don't have paper, I find repeating the information out loud to myself several times helps me imprint it in my Left brain so that I will remember the information later. I sometimes call myself and leave a message on my voice recorder.

When the insights come they need to be captured. Because we flow from the Right brain back to the Left brain for normal daily functions many times during the day, we sometimes forget the great insights we get from the Right brain unless we do write them down or reinforce them in our Left brain in some way as suggested above.

Some answers come quickly and some take a little time, but the search engine is still working on it even when you have gone back to Left brain dominance. In fact, sometimes you will ask a big question, get the answer a week or a month later, and forget you even asked the question. Be mindful of what you are asking for, and be mindful when the answer comes.

Act on the answers you get. I always add a little "Thank You!" when I get the answer. Appreciation and application of the information received encourages future performance in the brain and with others in life!

Life Experience:

Just the other day I asked myself, "How can I get a little more exercise in my daily activities instead of having to walk on the treadmill?"

The next day I had to go to the courthouse to get proof of a tax payment. I was told on the phone to go to the Registrar of Deeds. No problem - I knew right where that was; I had been there before. I parked in the parking ramp across the street from the court house and headed for the front of the building. When I got there, a notice in the window said that the Registrar of Deeds office had been moved to another building a block away.

So I walked over there and after waiting in line I was told that the information I needed was at the tax department, two blocks away. I walked over there and went to the first tax office I came to and was promptly told that I was not in the "right" tax office. So I continued to another part of the building to the right office.

When I reached that office, I was told that I really needed to go back to the Public Documents department, which was back at the court house! I walked the two blocks there and had to use the stairs to the correct office because the elevator was being serviced. After getting the document I needed, I then walked back across the street to the parking ramp and got in my car.

When I sat down in the car, I started laughing. I found out exactly how I could get a little more exercise in my daily activities without having to use the treadmill!

Set It Up

Instead of just going from one event, meeting, phone call, or project to another, take the time to set it up. When you run from one thing to another your attitude from one may spill into the other. Do you ever bring problems from home to work with you? Have you ever noticed that when the day starts out "bad," it usually continues and may even get worse?

The **Set It Up** process starts with: **Attitude and Expectation**

When you wake up in the morning, take a few minutes to think about what you are doing for the day. Set up your attitude for the day and your expectation. I often start with "I'm still here, which is a good thing; might as well make this a magical day!" When you get in your car decide the trip to work will be easy. When you have a meeting, take just a few minutes to think about what you want to accomplish and how you want to feel when the meeting is over. Do the same with phone calls and meals and whatever you are doing that day. Before going to sleep at night, set the expectation for restful and restorative sleep. Set the tone and the expectations in general for the day and specifically for each event.

Things might not always come out exactly as expected, but you have a far better chance of it happening that way than if you drift through the day oblivious to your attitude and having no expectations. That is creation or formation by default. You spend your day reacting to the environment instead of responding to your focus.

I have been traveling a great deal lately and I set up my expectations for perfect travel connections and car rentals a day or two before I leave.

On a recent trip, the flight connections were tight, but I kept thinking abut my expectations. It all happened as I had planned. When I arrived at my destination and went to the car rental place, I had set the expectation to get an SUV. Since that was not in the category that the company would pay for, it would have be a free upgrade.

There was a gentleman in front of me at the car rental desk. He was being very particular about what car he wanted and kept refusing the offer of the representative. I waited patiently. I was happy to be on the ground.

The gentleman kept hemming and hawing and the representative turned his attention to me. I explained that I had a reservation and wanted an SUV. He said it would cost me $5.00 extra per day and I declined.

The gentleman interrupted and asked for another car. The representative went to assist him, leaving me to wait again. I didn't mind because some other people had come in and we were all chatting and laughing.

The gentleman still was not satisfied with the cars available and the representative looked at me with exasperation written all over his face. I simply smiled.

The representative then said, "You know what? I'm going to give you your SUV as a free upgrade!" I, once again, only smiled and said a big, "Thank You!"

I smiled all the way to the car. My expectations had been met. I made all of my flight connections on the way home also.

Wake It Up

The Genius brain is the place to connect to infinite resources and infinite possibilities. Every resource available in the universe is available at this level of thinking. This is the place where focus, feeling, faith, and formation come together in one "Whole brain" space and time, and it is an extremely powerful process.

The Wake It Up process starts with:
Daydreaming on Steroids!

This process will take 15-20 minutes the first time and works best if done two times a day for approximately 10 minutes each time to be fully effective.

You will need to be in a quiet, private space that is comfortable and away from distractions. Read through these instructions once to grasp the idea, and then let it flow freely when you practice. I have chosen to personify the organization in general, but you can just focus on certain parts if that is your desire. Make this your daydream, your creation, your formation.

Start by sitting in a comfortable chair. I do not recommend lying down since your natural tendency in that position is to sleep. Close your eyes, and take several deep, cleansing, relaxing breaths in and out. Relax your mind and your body slowly and incrementally with each deep breath.

As you relax, sense a lush green landscape in your mind's eye and continue to relax more. You are looking at the verdant greenery, with the sun shining pleasantly and the temperature perfect. Notice that there is a path in front of you, and you are drawn to start walking down the path to an even deeper foliage area. As you go further down the path, you begin to hear the sound of water. It sounds like a waterfall is just ahead. The path is going down now, deeper and deeper into this beautiful, safe, and serene setting. The waterfall appears off to your right, and you are intrigued to follow the path deeper and deeper to get to the bottom of the waterfall. The path is an easy descent, and the sound and beauty of the waterfall is so relaxing.

Soon you reach the area where the waterfall ends at a pool of water. You stop for a moment and just watch the water falling into the pool. As you look closer, you notice that there is an easy way to get over to the edge, slip under the waterfall and actually sit under it. It is so inviting, the day is warm, you are safe, and you are alone in this wonderful piece of serenity.

You take off your clothes and leave them at the edge of the pond and slip into the water, under the waterfall, and sit on the ledge that seems made for just such an adventure. Even though the water is pouring over your head, you realize that it is easy to breath and the water is just the perfect temperature. You begin to relax so much more. The water seems to be cleansing you on the outside and the inside. It pours over your head, over your shoulders, down your arms, gliding down your chest and abdomen. It continues over your hips, down your legs and feet. As it goes down, it really does feel like all of your cares and worries are washed away. All of the burdens, aches and pains disappear as the water flows.

You feel so clean and this experience feels so decadent that you feel like a kid who snuck away to your own private hideout. You begin to kick your feet and hold your hands out so the water can splash around them. You begin to smile widely and to snicker a little. This is the life; you have found your own little piece of paradise!

You are really feeling adventurous now, and you move out into the pool and move around, splashing and floating. Eventually you move over to the edge and down the path a little more where the pool seems very calm. There seems to be another pool below that one as the water cascades down the hill. You climb up on a warm, flat rock in the sun to sit and dry off. You notice that the pool is so calm here that you can see reflections in the water.

You see the reflection of an athlete who has seen better days. He is frustrated and has some battle scars from many attempts to master his game. He once had aspirations of being a great runner and running the hurdles with ease. Now he seems to be stumbling on each hurdle, and the hurdles are all he can see. All of his systems, including respiratory, circulatory, nutritional, and nervous, systems once were in great shape; his mind was so clear and his spirit high. Everything once worked in such harmony then, but now he can't seem to make any of them work well, let alone make them work in harmony. He is at a loss to figure out what happened that got him here and is too exhausted and frustrated to see anything but the hurdles.

The reflection of this man, you realize, is a reflection of your business organization, and it makes you feel sad for a moment. As you look at the tiered pools, and the waterfall above, you decide to just let that reflection flow out of this pool and away. You watch it carefully to be sure that it all flows away, and as it does you feel relieved.

As you relax on the warm rock, you begin to ponder what it would be like if that athlete was really the Olympian he always wanted to be. You begin to see a different image of him reflecting in that pool. You see him at the track running the hurdles. You admire his strong body and the skill with which he manages the hurdles. He seems to fly over them with a beautiful, even stride honed with practice. His confidence is high and his vision is keen. He knows he is practicing to win the gold medal. All systems are working in harmony. You see the result of his dedication and skill in the way he is running. You see and can actually feel his determination and focus. Gold…Gold…Gold…Gold.

He is now at the starting line of the race. The crowd is cheering him on, his coach and trainers are there supporting him, the volunteers are cheering him on. His heart swells with pride and honor. He begins his race at the starting signal, his vision is clear about winning that gold medal and he knows that he can take any and all of those hurdles in his stride. He runs like the wind and crosses the finish line first. The crowd goes WILD; he is bursting with pride at accomplishing the goal.

When the media approaches him and asks him how he did it, he answers, "It was a team effort. It seemed like when I focused clearly, everyone lined up behind me to support the effort and with great synchronicity, it all came together. I did the running, but I had a lot of help from the team." And as he goes to the podium to get the gold medal, he thinks about all the doors this opens up for him, and the world looks very bright indeed.

You realize that this vision in the reflection pool is of your organization also, and this one you decide to keep. You walk down to the water's edge and put your left hand in the water palm up. You let that whole reflection concentrate into a ball and drift into your hand. You then move your left hand to your forehead and implant that vision in your "whole brain" as the creation that you will take with you.

You have a warm feeling and smile on your face as you decide it is time to gather your things and head back up the hill. This was such a great journey. You start up the hill with an easy stride, still enjoying the sound of the waterfall, but noticing that it seems different now. Now it seems exhilarating instead of relaxing. The higher you climb, the more rejuvenated you feel. You go higher and higher up the hill at an easy, yet energized pace. Up and up until you reach the top and look at the lush greenery once more. You take a long, deep breath, and you become aware of your body sitting in the chair where you started this journey. You begin to move your fingers and your toes as you bring your attention back into the room. You slowly open your eyes feeling more refreshed, more hopeful, more confident, and more determined to go for the gold for the team.

*****

When you do this process in the future two times a day, you do not need to see the reflection of the man that was failing; that reflection was washed away by the waterfall. Just picture the star athlete and winner of the gold medal.

Using the Olympic athlete is just a suggestion. Whatever vision you can hold of success and achievement for the organization is fine. You can put as much detail into the vision as you can while "feeling" empowered and enthused. If the good feeling is not in the vision, then pick something that evokes that feeling and hold it for several minutes. Hold the vision of potential and great eagerness.

Note: During the 2 months I was focused on writing, rewriting and editing this portion of the book, my center made production goals for the first time in several months. Coincidence? Hmmm…

. . . .

CHAPTER 5

Developing Focus, Feelings and Faith

One of my "just curious" questions at the Right brain level was, "What language does the Universe converse in?"

There are so many languages in this world, we are all asking questions in some way or another, and I wanted to know the common denominator. The answer seemed very simple as it came to me in the shower one morning.

The Universe converses in pictures and emotions. Have you ever watched the news and seen events from across the world? Even if you don't speak the language of the people in disastrous events, can you recognize the emotions of anguish, fear, anger, pain, regret, confusion, and frustration in the faces of those involved? Can you recognize a joyous event and see the expressions of joy, elation, fun, laughter, love, and gratitude on the faces of these people even when you don't understand their language?

Even when you are in familiar territory and speak the same language, have you ever walked into a room and instantly recognized the "energy" or atmosphere of the room and the moods of the people in it without anyone saying a word?

There are pictures and emotions, internal or external, in all of life's events; some subtle and some obvious.

According to A. Barbour, author of *Louder Than Words: Nonverbal Communication*, it is broken down like this for humans:

7 percent verbal (words)

38 percent vocal (volume, pitch, rhythm, etc)

55 percent body movements (mostly facial expressions)

We observe situations much like we observe verbal and nonverbal communication. The universal energy speaks to us in pictures and emotions subtly. We have to be in the state of mind to receive them, as discussed earlier. And if we are to speak the language of the universal energy, we must learn to be clearer in our pictures and our emotions and not rely so heavily on our words. We've been born with the ability to think and feel. We need to use this knowledge to our advantage, take responsibility for creating our own pictures and emotions, and not be simply immersed in the pictures and emotions created by others.

Focus: The Thoughts, Mental Attitudes and Pictures

It would seem that building focus would be easy, but it is not always so. When I ask some people in their current job what they want to be doing 20 years from now, they usually say something like, "not this." They mean they want to progress to another position or go back to school or get experience in a different area within the current organization or another. Their focus, however, is on "not this". Their focus is on what they don't want instead of directly on what they do want, literally running away from something they don't want rather than running toward something they do want.

Let me ask you, what pictures, mental attitudes or thoughts come to mind when you get an answer like, "not this" in regard to a question about what they want in their career path?

- Nothing,

- Something very vague,

- Something negative.

- Those picturing nothing are living by default, having chosen nothing to focus on and just putting in the hours to get paid.

- Those who have a vague picture are hoping something will change, but not doing anything to change it.

- Those who have a negative picture are unhappy themselves and often create a negative picture for others.

So if you want to create by design, and change your life and your organization, you need to get clear on the focus. Paint as vivid a picture as you can when you desire something. Put yourself in the picture. Don't just leave it somewhere "out there" in front of you like the proverbial carrot. You will never get it unless you bring it in to you, engaging your Whole brain while being an active part of it.

Life Experience:

The "paint the vivid picture" expression sometimes frustrated me because I am a *visual person* when functioning primarily in my Left brain, but I am a *sensual person* in my Right brain. What that means is, I could not "see" visually at the alpha brain wave level or Right brain. I could only "sense" a picture of the idea and create a mental attitude that would lead me to an emotional feeling.

I had to write down my desires in as much detail as possible and use words that expressed my feelings as well. It put my desires in my Whole brain in a different way than just thinking and trying to "see" my desires. The act of writing is Left brain, the act of picturing with emotion is Right brain. The act of putting the two together in a daydreaming state magnifies the focus of the desire and creates the clarity needed.

Weather you "see" or "sense," it is OK as long as it leads you to the desired state you are reaching for. For example: If you want to develop a "can do" attitude in your place of business, you may not have a physical picture of it, but you can sense the change in energy and attitudes of people in the workplace; something like sensing a lighter energy when you walk in the door, hearing laughter or a lilt in someone's voice, "seeing/ sensing" smiles on generic faces rather than specific faces. It is a general mental attitude, a set of beliefs and focused thoughts that you want to sense.

So the focus can be something you "see" or something you "sense." If the desire is strong and you know "what" you want, how it "appears" is simply the way you perceive it.

Feelings: The Emotional Attitudes Evoked by the Desire

The feelings about your desires may come easy for you and they may not. I hear people say that they cannot help how they feel. Feelings are emotions attached to events or words and are learned reactions or responses. If they were learned, they can be changed.

Our environment, culture, parents, teachers, and preachers teach us how to react and respond to certain events and words. For example, in some cultures the death of a child is considered horrible and painful. In some cultures, however, the death of a child means that the child has learned the life experience it came to learn and their death releases them to a higher spiritual plane. Their death is celebrated and rejoiced.

Emotions can be so powerful and instantaneous that for some, "choosing" a feeling can be a strange and uncomfortable experience and seemingly impossible at times. It can be done by simply "being aware" of your reactions to certain events or stimuli. With awareness then, the emotion can be changed to something more appropriate. It may mean leaving your comfort zone and creating a new perspective, but it will also empower you. Ask questions of yourself when you have a strong feeling about something. For example: Is this feeling serving me? Do I want to change this feeling? What feeling would fit this situation better and serve me?

Life Experience:

I grew up in a family of stoic women who had come through wars, tough financial times and single parent dilemmas. They had grown a really "tough emotional skin" and dismissed their own feelings as useless. Once again, we all learn from our parents, teachers and preachers, and environmental influences.

Some might say that I was aloof because I was taught not to honor my feelings; actually taught to ignore them. Regardless of my upbringing, I, however, was feeling a lot of things but did not know how to express them.

And in addition to my upbringing, after much introspection, I remembered shutting down my feelings when I went through the trauma of being raped.

I decided to change my feelings about it through my awareness. It was a turning point in my life and why I have studied "how life works." I have been able to see the treasure in the trauma now. I have learned how to express my feeling now.

You may need to assess how you feel about the things you desire. Get in touch with your authentic feelings and let yourself feel the ups as well as the downs. You can only go as high as you are willing to go low when it comes to feelings. Go low and feel those feelings of sadness, knowing that all feelings are temporary. Then let go of the low feelings and be free to go high and feel the joys.

Part of the creation formula is to add feelings to your focus. Obviously you want those feeling to be positive and as heartfelt as you can muster! Feelings are energy, and we live in an energy Universe. You need to know how you are feeling just as much as you need to know what you are thinking and focusing on. The purpose of focus and feeling is to direct the vibrational, creative energy in the direction of "your" desires so that you can create by design and not continually by default.

The underlying emotional attitude in your desire is a critical part of making a change. We each have "customary" emotional attitudes or comfort zones in which we handle daily events. Are you a glass half full or half empty kind of person? Are problems roadblocks and hurdles, or are they opportunities and catalysts for change? Which do you think will direct your energy best when focusing on your desire?

Emotional attitudes as well as mental attitudes are your choice.

As we have discussed, we have adopted our attitudes from our parents, teachers and preachers, customs, and cultures. This, without examination on your part, is default thinking and feeling. You can make a choice in these attitudes once you become aware that you have a choice.

Your focus or desire is given energy by your feelings and emotions, so to create by design, to create a change; it must be made a part of your daily life. Changing things will probably not happen over night. You have practiced that comfort zone for a long time, and it will take some effort on your part to allow yourself a new comfort zone, a new perspective. As you use these techniques and apply this new knowledge consistently, change will occur. The mirror will show a different image.

Faith: Believing Before Seeing

Belief and trust must be built. Just because the Left brain is the logical, realist does not mean that it sees things clearly or as they really are. We all "see" things through our own filters of experience, knowledge, and influences.

We all look through our own lenses as if they were contact lenses. If you are looking through yellow lenses, everything in the world will look yellow to you. You will swear that yellow is the truth of the situation, the world, and the Universe because it is the norm for you. If someone hands you a pair of blue lenses and you are willing to put them on, first you think it is crazy and you may take them off immediately because it is uncomfortable for you to venture outside of your yellow comfort zone. After all, you believe that is the truth. If you wear the blue lenses for a period of time, however, blue becomes your new truth and your new norm. Changing your norm in the way you see things is uncomfortable but possible given time and desire.

We believe what we see and say "I'll believe it when I see it" when confronted with new ideas and perspectives. However, there is always an underlying belief to any image. There is a belief that the Left brain, full of logic and probabilities, is the only one that "sees" the "true" picture. That is physical sight and is based on the mirror of thought and emotions already in place.

Faith is the sight of the Right brain called "insight." It creates the sight through a connection with the Right brain and the Genius brain. Faith is an internal belief in our own power, not the power of others. The lenses that were developed by default from our association with others may or may not be the vision we carry within ourselves.

Our own power comes from our vision, our emotion and our faith and no one else's. That is what we must learn to harness to complete the creation process. We must know our own power and trust it. We must listen or sense our own insight and take "inspired" action as a result of it. This Right/Genius brain insight creates the new mirror images that the Left can "see."

Building Faith in Our Own Power
The Show Me Test

Whenever I doubt my ability to create, I go back to the simplest of things. I start on small, inconsequential things that would just be fun to create and "see" results. The more often you do this, the more belief you have in your own power and the easier it is to create a more important experience in your life.

Start by thinking of something small you want to see, feel, hear, or read in the next few days. Make it something that is so odd and fun that you will be delighted when it appears and it will be impossible to deny. Just think about it a few times and let it go to your Right brain with a "create it and show me" kind of attitude. Suspend disbelief for the time being. This is fun!

Life Experience:

I decided I wanted to see someone with pink hair, odd enough that I would notice and silly enough for the "show me" test. I sent the request to the Right brain and let it go. I had almost forgotten the test when a week later a customer walked in with pink hair. I almost burst out laughing with delight.

I decided I wanted to see, hear, or read about a marble: once again a word or sight you don't see everyday.

The next day I picked up a crossword puzzle during a break at work and the first clue my eyes were drawn to was "a five letter word for marble".

I decided to test further. On my way to a major store, I decided I wanted a close-to-the-door parking space. When I pulled in there was someone just pulling out of the first space, which I took as I smiled widely.

I went to an event that had thousands of people from all over the world attending. I knew a couple from another state that were coming to the event and when I spoke with them on the phone, I simply said, "I'll see you there." They laughed and said it was unlikely since there were so many people attending and it spread over several buildings. I went to the event and a few hours into it, I was heading up an escalator and those skeptical friends were heading down the escalator. They were surprised and I was delighted as I gave them an "I told you so" wink.

I was flying home every 6 weeks or so during my first year of a new job in another state. I carried my little dog with me each time. The connecting flights always seemed to be at the other end of the same terminal or in a totally different terminal. That little 10 pound dog felt like it weighed 50 pounds after the long walk. I decided to try an experiment, another test to see how good I was at this creation thing. Before I left I thought about the connecting gate being within 10 gates of the incoming gate and let it go with a picture in my brain and an expectant feeling. It happened! So on the journey home, bolstered by success, I thought about the gates being within 8 of each other and it happened! The next time I traveled I decided on only 5 gates separating the incoming and outgoing gates. It happened again and so I challenged with 2 gates between and it happened. Now what? Did I dare push it and go for 1? I did. I came in on 5A and went out on 5B! I was so excited I could hardly contain myself.

Building your faith is critical to creation/formation. We do, however, have to take off the Left brain lenses and put on the lenses of the Right brain for this to succeed. The Left brain "but" and focus on probabilities can derail our creation. The Right brain "and" and focus on possibilities is necessary to let the creation happen.

In order to engage the Right and Left brain, you can decide to use the Monocle of Miracles. The Left brain can keep one lens and the Right brain can have the other lens. It is a much more balanced and Whole brain approach to life.

This means that you can keep one eye on probabilities and one eye on possibilities. You can keep one eye on performance and one eye on potential. You can keep one eye on the current formation in front of you and one eye on the vision of the formation in progress.

You are continually creating tomorrow with your focus and feelings of today, in fact, at this very this moment! Wouldn't you want to have at least one eye on the vision at all times? Look for the evidence of change in focus; feel for the evidence of change in attitude each and every day. You will begin to see new mirrors show up in your life. Begin to question how you look and feel about the things around you.

- **Creation Formula: Focus + Feelings + Faith= Formation**

Do not go where the path may lead...go instead where there is no path and leave a trail.

Ralph Waldo Emerson

CHAPTER 6

Refining Goals and Measurements

Vision without action is a daydream.

Action without vision is a nightmare.

Japanese Proverb

The goals of many organizations are so lofty or written in a way that the average employee cannot relate to them. When writing goals and job descriptions in the different positions I have held, I had to write them to please the MBA's and PhD's.

- To be the preeminent provider of xyz...

- To present a deeper understanding of xyz...

- To establish a greater presence of xyz...

When I later asked employees what they meant, I received the "deer in the headlight" look. They had no idea how these goals related to their position and what they were supposed to do to meet these goals. I would then have to "translate" them so they would truly understand what the goals of the organization were and how their job descriptions related to them.

Many organizations break down the lofty goals into strategic plans or initiatives, and those should be relatable to most employees. Sometimes they are, and sometimes they are not.

Most goals are flat and one-dimensional to me. There does not seem to be any energy in the goals, and they are strictly Left brain activities. They are words on a page that serve the practicality of the Left brain. However, to put action in anything, the Right brain needs to be stimulated also to stir emotion and create movement. Motivation means the Motive for Action. Goals need to be written in a way to indicate the motive or why employees are asked to do certain things *and* what action needs to be taken to accomplish the goals.

I have found that the Motive + the Action were still not enough to engage some employees. Emotion was the missing component. That is why I created a process and tried it with a group of 30 frontline supervisors and sales people in one organization. The process was intended to engage the Left brain and the Right brain. I made it logical, creative *and* fun!

Wild Wacky Wishes

I chose specific terms within the organization that related to everyday goals and tasks. I asked the group to start creating the Wild Wacky Wishes working in groups of 3 to 4 people. I made it even more fun by having them write the Wild Wacky Wishes on Pretty Purple Paper. The Wild Wacky Wishes had to be three words long and all had to start with the same letter or at least sound.

It became so much fun that I had to rein them in a few times. I strolled through the room to see how they were doing and I heard someone coming up with Lovely Luscious Lips. Redirecting them to the business related focus, they created some great ones specific to our industry!

The Left brain focuses on the goal or business related task/term, and the Right brain creates the action and/or the emotion evoking word. It brings life and energy to the words and the goals.

Focus + Feeling = Formation.

- The Left brain creates the focus,

- The Right brain creates the fun or movement,

- Formation is the result.

I have picked some generic topics to show you some examples.

Topic: Customer Service

Creative Customer Cervice (Literary License!)

Caring Customer Connections

Creating Customer Comfort

Consumer Coaching Connections

Capturing Customer Choices

Topic: Financial Success

Flourishing Funds Flowing

Financial Funds Forever

Money Magnet Modifications

Millionaire Money Mindset

Financial Fortune Forming

Topic: Compliance

Compliance Culture Cresting

Creating Compliance Culture

Coordinating Compliance Controls

Compliance Consequences Comprehended

Compliance Compact Created

Topic: Miscellaneous

Prosperous Product Purchasers

Perfectly Pleased People

Creative Cost Controls

Making Multi Millionaires

Building Brotherhood Bonds

Simply Superb Services

You get the idea. Use a dictionary if necessary to keep the Left brain happy and then ask questions of the Right brain. What word fits the criteria and makes a statement? What word conveys the feeling of the goal? What word puts action into the goal?

Notice that your eyes go up a few degrees and possibly back and forth searching for the right word. A thesaurus can help if the Left brain really gets stuck, but it is fun to create the Wild Wacky Wishes and especially fun if you work in a group and brainstorm them.

You are engaging both the Left and Right brain and Focusing with Feeling on the goals of the business. It creates an energy that moves things in the right direction. Focus + Feeling driving the Formation.

Measurements

I invented my life by taking for granted that everything I did not like would have an opposite, which I would like.

Coco Chanel

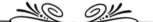

Every organization has to measure its progress in some way. It can measure its successes or its failures. What I have seen in many organizations is an intention to measure successes when their systems are actually measuring their failures.

If you are measuring compliance, you are expecting the people in the organization to function at their highest level without making errors. If we apply the Focus + Feeling formula to this, you will be able to see that one way you measure compliance actually gets more of what you want and another way of measuring compliance can get you more of what you don't want.

Let me illustrate with a picture: There is a big beautiful estate with a massive manicured lawn, lush plantings, fertile ground, inviting paths, and alluring fragrances. There is also a muddy ditch in front of the property along the roadway. An employee is standing on the roadway, and you are having a conversation with him or her about the view.

If you and the organizational measurements are focused on the beautiful scene in front of you and you point out the 98% of what is beautiful and productive, then you are really focused on compliance and encouraging more of the same.

If, on the other hand, you and the organizational measurements are focused on the mud in the ditch and the 2% of problems, then you are focused on the problems and the mud and inadvertently encouraging more of the same by the focus of the conversation.

If you tell an employee they are standing in 2% mud and you want them to reduce that to 1% within a given time, they have no idea how to be standing in less mud! Do they climb the ditch, do they fill it in? What do *you* want that person to do?

Instead of asking them to produce more of a desirable, you are asking them to produce less of an undesirable. Where the attention goes, the energy goes. Do you really want an employee focusing all their attention on climbing out of the ditch and the undesirable?

We live in a world where people want more, not less. It is counter-intuitive to ask someone to produce fewer problems or stand in less mud! They are focused on the problems and have to individually decide what you really want and how to accomplish that.

If, on the other hand, they were told they have a 98% compliance rate and you appreciate their work in creating this beautiful landscape, you have now nurtured and fertilized more compliance. If you would like them to have a 99% compliance rate within a given time frame, they can now focus on what they have already created and create more of it. They will focus on the green grass, the lush greenery, the beauty that they are already producing and be so busy doing so that they simply avoid the muddy ditch.

If the focus is really on compliance then all measurements would indicate the appreciation of the desired result instead of the undesirable result. Of course, the employee needs to know what his or her problems are so he or she can then focus on understanding, correcting, adjusting, and then refocusing his or her efforts on the desired result - performance management vs. problem management.

Note: During the week that I was focused on writing and editing this portion and, I had two problems logged on me. I had no problems in the previous 8 months. Coincidence? Hmmm…

CHAPTER 7

The Focus Forum

Where two or more are gathered...

People love to tell their story. Sometimes they tell them to get sympathy, and sometimes they want to get a laugh and sometimes they just want to vent.

Have you ever noticed in your organization what the topics of conversation occur when people gather? Do you find that one person starts with a story and the next person chimes in with his or her own similar story, but tries to top the other person in the drama or severity of what happened? If there are more people involved, more people chime in with their tales of woe or disaster and the conversation is all focused on "what is going wrong."

These conversations, small and large, happen on breaks, lunches, meetings or just passing in the hall. People want to share their story, but in organizations, it is often a negatively focused conversation.

What is really happening? The Formation process is happening all of the time. Focus + Feelings = Formation. While Faith is needed for desired Future Formation, it is not a conscious event in these conversations; they already have proof of what their Formation is. They are seeing and living the mirror image of their creation.

They are already experiencing what is going wrong, and in the process of continuing to discuss that day in and day out, they create even more without knowing it.

When people are focused on negative events or circumstances and then add feelings of drama or humor, fully believing every word, they are

unknowingly forming or creating more of the
same events or circumstances in the future.

You can get caught up in these kind of conversations
all the time if you are not hyper-alert!

Let me put this in a visual. You are having a
conversation with someone I call a "vacuum cleaner."
They present the dirt and suck you in. You add your
own dirt and get sucked in further. Others add their
dirt and get sucked in too. Everyone ends up in the "dirt
bag!" How does it make you feel when you walk away?
Do you feel good, or do you feel drained? Do you just
want to shake off the dirt and forget it happened? Or
do you just walk away wearing the dirt and take it with
you into your next conversation?

When you and the others are in that conversation,
it is unconscious negative creation at its finest. Out of
ignorance of energetic intelligence, you and they are
creating more of what is not wanted and in a powerful way.

We have all found ourselves wrapped up in a
conversation that is going in that negative direction.

If you are more aware of your feelings and thoughts in those moments, you can change the direction of the energy and change the direction of the creation, however. I spend a lot of time doing this. I call it redirecting.

People are so very clear on what they don't want, but often are at a loss for words when trying to explain what they do want. It is important to be able to articulate clearly what you do want, and it is often easier to do with another person or a group. Two heads are better than one. The sum total of the whole equals more than the sum total of its parts. That is why we have committees for so many things in the business world.

The Focus Forum is a place to brainstorm, not blamestorm. It is a place where members focus on what is going right and how you can create more of that. It is the place to be looking at and feeling for the potential. It is a forum where members talk about the collective vision, the forum where everyone adds parts to the vision to complete the whole. It creates harmony and a common bond; it creates focus, feeling, and faith, and it accelerates the formation.

The forum is the place to celebrate even small victories and build on those feelings that take the group in the direction of the vision. It is the place to be creating Wild Wacky Wishes!

Start the meeting with, "You are all great; give yourselves a round of applause!" It puts a smile on everyone's face and lightens the mood and changes the energy! For years I have, intuitively, clapped my hands in front of my face to change my thoughts and mood to something more positive. It creates an energy that is stimulating and uplifting and breaks the trance of default and/or negative thinking.

Find someone or some group that you can create with. Keep the focus positive and on the vision or creation desired. Clap for great ideas! Hint – they are all great ideas! They may or may not be probabilities or even possibilities, but they open the flow of communication between the Left brain, Right brain and Genius states of mind. They are all great ideas! Keep them flowing.

Meeting on a regular basis helps to keep the vision alive, the energy positive, and the faith high as you celebrate successes, and it speeds the formations. We live in a predominantly Left-brained world and we need to train ourselves to function as a Whole-brained person. Having the support of forum members makes it easier to keep the momentum going.

CHAPTER 8

Insight on Intention

While I was writing this book I had to face a lot of interesting things about myself. I have been "trying" to write this book for years. Something was always holding me back. I experienced self-sabotage to the maximum, procrastination and fear. No matter how many people would tell me, "You should write a book with all of that knowledge," I couldn't get it done. I would write, but it always sounded like "blah, blah, blah" flat, monotone, one-dimensional words when I read it.

One day before a meditation, I asked my Genius mind to give me some insight into what was happening. I have so much passion, but I write factually. What do I need to know to get the passion expressed in my work?

I sat down and listened to music that "transported" me to the mountains and a lovely cottage. I sat on the front porch in a rocking chair and just took in the beautiful scenery and sounds. I sat for some time doing that and suddenly someone was talking to me. I looked around, but did not see anyone. I "heard" in my head "just listen" and so I did. I was told that fear was holding me back. I questioned that. I wasn't aware of any fear that would hold me back. I had never actually written a book and it seemed daunting, but I had tried already and that fear didn't seem so big that it would hold me back.

At that point I was told the "real" fear. This voice said, "You were strangled within moments of losing your life for expressing your deepest emotions when you were raped. You silenced your emotions and ability to express your feelings in order to live."

At that moment a "ball of energy" burst within me like a popping beach ball. My eyes flew open and I came out of that meditation with a jolt! No wonder I could not write with passion and express my feelings. I felt like my life would be threatened if I expressed my powerful emotions.

- No wonder I would "choke" up when deep feelings emerged,

- No wonder I had laryngitis so many times in my life,

- No wonder that my tonsils became so infected that, strange as it may sound, I actually coughed one out,

- No wonder I can't wear anything tight around my neck,

- No wonder I currently have a low functioning thyroid!

What you don't know or won't face about yourself controls your life.

I had an experience recently when I woke up one morning with all kinds of fears rolling around in my head. Even my dreams had contained fears during the night. No amount of rationalizing about these fears would release them and the tightness in my "gut." In a fit of exasperation, I put my hands out in front of me in a motion of offering the fears to my Genius mind and said "Show me how to get rid of these."

A few minutes later, I was washing my face and I could hear a song in my head. The song was the theme song of the Monk TV series. I don't know if you are familiar with it, but the song is, "It's a Jungle Out There" written by Randy Newman. Adrian Monk, a brilliant detective, can hardly function in life because of "hilarious" and "irrational" fears. His brilliance cannot be shared freely because of his massive fears to almost everything in life. I started laughing, which by the way, is a great way to release the tension of fears. I was still laughing as I was writing these words.

Joe Vitale, author of the NY Times Best Selling book *"The Attractor Factor"* calls these beliefs, fears and past issues, counter-intentions. He has many ways to clear these in this book and in another called *"The Key"*.

The point is that counter-intentions can be so strong and even feel "life threatening in my case" that they keep you from creating what you really desire.

Are there counter-intentions that are keeping you from being a Quantum Leader?

I see things differently when looking at my own experiences. One day in my late teens, I went to the lake with friends. One of the guys was going to teach my roommate and me how to water ski. She was tall, thin and the athletic type. I was and am the soft, round and studious type.

She was going to go first, and I listened very carefully to the instructions she was given and I practiced them in my head over and over so when it was my turn, I would be great. The only instructions I heard were how to get up on the skis, and because it took her multiple tries, I got to hear the instructions several times. When she finally got up, she had a great time. While she was out there on the lake skiing away, I was on the shore waving and practicing in my head. When it came time for her to come back to shore, she easily drifted in and stood in the shallow water taking off her skis.

I hadn't been taught to do the drifting in part yet, but it looked simple enough. Great, I've got this, I thought. So it was now my turn. I held the rope just right and kept my knees together and leaned back AND I WAS UP ON THE FIRST TRY! I was skiing away and enjoying it and then....... another boat came by and left a wake that knocked me off balance and .... down I went.

Now all of you that have water skied are saying, "no big deal." So here's the problem. I had not been given any instructions about what to do if I fell. I'm the studious one and I LIKE instructions. Now I think those in the boat were probably shouting instructions at that point, but I could not hear them.

Do you know why I could not hear them? Because I was doing the serpentine thing behind the boat: hanging on to the rope for dear life. I was going up and down and twisting and turning, gasping for air, swallowing large amounts of dirty lake water, and I guess, waiting for instructions!

In my growing exhaustion it FINALLY occurred to me, LET GO OF THE ROPE! I found myself bobbing in turbulent water for a few minutes and then it calmed and I simply waited for the boat to come and pick me up.

Now, HOW MUCH EASIER would it have been if I had used my instincts instead of waiting for instructions? HOW MUCH EASIER would it have been if I had immediately let go of a rope that was not serving me any longer? HOW MUCH EASIER would it have been if I let go of the rope earlier and not waited until I was exhausted, swallowing so much dirty lake water and gasping for breath just to survive?

Now, every place I put ROPE in the story above I want you to substitute BELIEF or FEAR. HOW MUCH EASIER could your life be or your job be if you were willing to let go of the debilitating beliefs and fears and grasp on to a different rope or belief? HOW MUCH EASIER would it be if you let go of the rope and floated in the calm water for a while and allowed the boat (read Genius mind) to come pick you up? How much energy could you save, how much dirty water could you avoid, and how much easier would it be to breathe?

When you expect everything in life to have an instruction manual, you are creating by default, by someone else's creation. Are you holding on to other's beliefs and creations? Are you also holding on to your own beliefs that are not serving you? Are you holding on to fears that are actually counter-intentional?

It is critical to become aware of your own experiences on a regular basis and be willing to question whether your beliefs are helping or hindering your growth and your leadership ability. Do you have fears that hold you back from truly expressing who you are as a leader? Gaining insight into yourself and your beliefs frees you to move into your power and open the bridges between the Left brain, the Right brain and the Genius mind.

FOCUS + FEELING + FAITH = FORMATION

- FOCUS = thoughts and visions

- FEELINGS = attitudes and emotions

- FAITH = beliefs and knowing

- FORMATION = out-pictured result

- FOCUS with <u>DESIGNED</u> INTENTION,

- FEEL with <u>DESIGNED</u> INTENTION,

- HAVE FAITH with <u>DESIGNED</u> INTENTION

- FORM with <u>DESIGNED</u> INTENTION!

Let go of the ropes that bind you.

A Bag of Tools

Isn't it strange that princes and kings,

And clowns that caper in sawdust rings,

And common people like you and me

Are builders of eternity?

Each is given a bag of tools,

A shapeless mass, a book of rules"

And each must make – ere life is flown –

A stumbling block, or a stepping stone.

R. L. Sharpe

CHAPTER 9

Conclusion

"What we achieve inwardly will change outer reality."

Plutarch 46-120AD, Greek Essayist

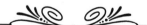

*"If you could kick the person in the pants
responsible for most of your trouble, you
wouldn't be able to sit for a month."*

Theodore Roosevelt, 26th President
of the United States

Business leaders, individually and as a group, have a far reaching impact on the lives of many. The financial impact of success and/or failure of a business can be felt to some degree world-wide. Each leader is responsible locally and globally to conduct business with integrity, with focus, with passion and with faith. Enlightenment to the Energies of the Universe and the direct engagement of the Genius Mind seem to be critical for the future of business success on this changing Earth.

To each of you reading this book;

This is your career, your choice, your chance to become a Quantum Leader and make an enlightened contribution to the World and the Universe.

RECOMMENDED READING

Daring:

Braden, Gregg. *The Spontaneous Healing of Belief*
Shattering the Paradigm of False Limits

More Daring:

Dooley, Mike. *Infinite Possibilities* The Art of Living
Your Dreams

Even More Daring

Vitale, Joe. *The Attractor Factor* 5 Easy Steps for
Creating Wealth (or Anything Else) from the Inside Out

Hold on to Your Hat Daring:

Hicks, Esther and Jerry (The Teachings of Abraham).
Ask and it is Given Learning to Manifest Your Desires